The
Roadside
Guide to
Bike
Repairs

The Roadside Guide to Bike Repairs

By Dennis Coello

Ross Books   Berkeley, Calif.

ISBN 0-89496-041-5

My thanks again for the artwork of Dennis Nieweg and Mary Perkins. Nate Bischoff provided two of the mechanical drawings, along with all of the comic sketches. And a special note of gratitude to my three artist friends for putting up with my constant pleas to hurriedly complete their work.

Dedication:

I dedicate this book to my former students of Rowland Hall-St. Mark's School, and all my other friends who over the years have asked me to help them fix their bikes. Your broken spokes and derailleur problems, and especially your questions, have been a great impetus for this endeavor. Now I can simply hand you this guide, wish you luck, and spend my time biking in the mountains.

Introduction

This simple guide to bicycle mechanics is designed for anyone who winces at the thought of a flat tire. It is made for the person who has heard of ball bearings but isn't quite sure of their purpose. And it is intended for those folks who, though they might already know which end of a wrench does the work, are yet unsure of what to do with it when it comes to a bike. I have kept this guide short so that its weight and size will allow you to take it along on rides. Despite its brevity, however, it contains everything I have learned about bicycle maintenance and repair since my first cross-country ride in 1965. Eight major tours and an around-the-world ride in the interim have made experience my teacher of mechanics. And living for the past six years without an automobile, commuting to and from work and caring for my wife's bike and mine, has given me a good taste of repairs necessitated by city streets.

Rising fuel prices are putting people back on two wheels, but bike shop repair fees have also gone up. With a small cash outlay for tools, however, you'll be able to avoid these repair costs as well. Take your time, learn the basics in repairs and maintenance, and you'll never have to worry about breakdowns or repair bills again. This book and a bit of patience make up a sure way to keep you, your bike, and your wallet in good shape.

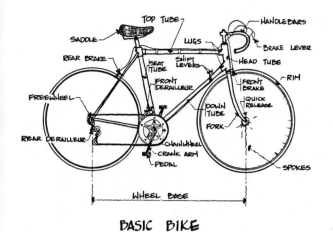

SADDLE — TOP TUBE — HANDLEBARS
LUGS — BRAKE LEVER
REAR BRAKE — HEAD TUBE
SEAT TUBE — SHIFT LEVERS
FRONT DERAILLEUR — FRONT BRAKE — RIM
FREEWHEEL — DOWN TUBE — QUICK RELEASE
REAR DERAILLEUR — FORK
CHAINWHEEL
CRANK ARM
PEDAL — SPOKES

WHEEL BASE

BASIC BIKE

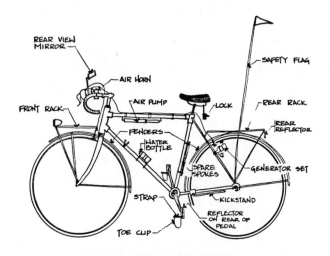

REAR VIEW MIRROR
AIR HORN — SAFETY FLAG
FRONT RACK — AIR PUMP — LOCK — REAR RACK
FENDERS — REAR REFLECTOR
WATER BOTTLE
SPARE SPOKES — GENERATOR SET
STRAP — KICKSTAND
REFLECTOR ON REAR OF PEDAL
TOE CLIP

COMMUTING BIKE

Table of Contents

1. *Tools / 11*
2. *Saddle / 19*
    1. Height / 20
    2. Tilt / 21
    3. Forward & backward movement / 22
    4. Side-to-side movement / 22
3. *Handlebars and Headsets / 25*
    1. Loose bars / 25
    2. Loose brake lever / 27
    3. New bar tape / 28
    4. Bars difficult to turn from side to side / 29
    5. Raising and lowering the bars / 30
4. *Wheels / 33*
    1. Flats / 33
    2. Wheel alignment / 39
    3. Broken spokes / 44
    4. Wheel bearing maintenance / 46
    5. Freewheel removal / 51
5. *Crank Assemblies / 55*
    Cotterless / 55
    Cotterpin / 58
6. *Pedals / 61*
7. *Brakes / 63*
    1. Cable adjustment / 64
    2. Cable replacement / 65
    3. Brake pads / 67
8. *Derailleurs / 71*
    Rear derailleur / 71
    Front derailleur / 80
9. *Chains / 85*
10. *Accessory Attachments / 91*
    1. Fenders / 91
    2. Racks / 92
    3. Flag / 94
    4. Generator Light / 94
    5. Toe clips & straps / 95
    6. Kickstand / 95
    7. Water Bottles / 95
Appendix: Bicycle Mail Order Catalogues / 99

1.

In this section I will list the tools I have accumulated over the years and which I find necessary or helpful in maintaining my bike. I will add current costs as averaged from three or more bicycle catalogues, or as determined locally in bike shops and hardware stores. (I have included the names and addresses of mail order catalogues in the Appendix.) I will indicate if I use the tool at home, carry it with me while commuting, or take it on tour. Finally, a list of the repairs or components for which these individual tools are necessary will be provided. (Where more than one tool will serve the purpose, I will indicate my personal preference.)

1. Crescent wrench 6" - $6
   a) Uses - saddle, handlebars, wheel axle nuts, cotterless crank, brakes, derailleurs, pedal removal
   b) Home, commuting, touring

2. Crescent wrench 4" - $4.50
   a) Uses - easier to use with brakes than 6" due to smaller size, same is true for derailleurs
   b) Home, commuting

3. Regular blade screwdriver - overall length 6", blade tip 3/16" wide - $2
   a) Uses - tightening brake lever bolts on handlebars, handlebar end plugs, prying out dust caps over bearing cups, backing out pedal cones, derailleur adjustment
   b) Home, commuting, touring

4. Needle-nose pliers, smallest available with side-cutters - $4
   a) Uses - pulling cables taut during replacement, cutting cables to length
   b) Home, commuting, touring

5. Channel locks 7" - $6.50
   a) Uses - pedal dust caps, headset, freewheel removal on road
   b) Home, commuting, touring

6. Tire levers - $1.50 for two
   a) Uses - fix flats
   b) Home, commuting, touring

7. Allen wrenches - 75 cents apiece
   a) Uses - chainring bolts, derailleur pivot bolts, crankarm dust caps, some saddles and handlebars
   b) Home, commuting, touring

8. Cone wrenches - two (13 & 14mm, 15 & 16mm) $2.50 per pair
   a) Uses - wheel bearing cone adjustment
   b) Home, commuting, touring

9. Chain rivet tool - $3.50
   a) Uses - chain removal and replacement, freeing frozen links
   b) Home, commuting, touring

10. Spoke nipple wrench "T-type" - 75 cents
    a) Uses - spokes
    b) Home, commuting, touring

11. Freewheel tool - Sun Tour $2, most others approximately $5
    a) Uses - freewheel removal
    b) Home, commuting touring

12. Cotterless crank removal tool - $4 to $8
    a) Uses - crank removal
    b) Home, commuting, touring

13. Universal cotterless crank wrench - $11.50 (optional)
    a) Uses - removal of crank arm fixing bolt (Same as removal tool above, but made to fit all crank bolts. I have one only because of the many different bikes I service.)
    b) Home

14. Universal cotterless crank arm puller - $10 (optional)
    a) Uses - pulls crank arms (my reason for

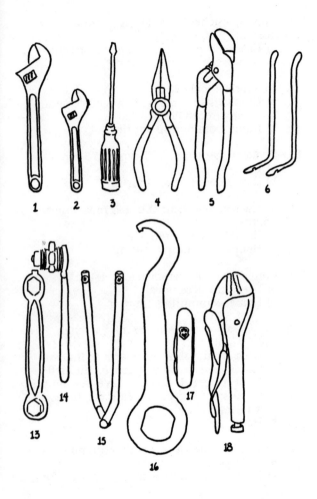

1

2

3

4

5

6

13

14

15

16

17

18

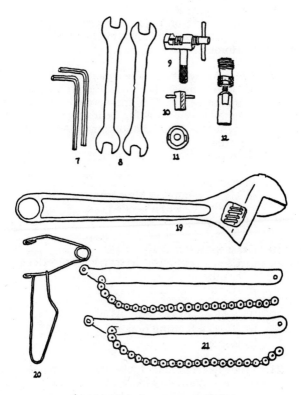

having this is same as above)
b) Home

15. Universal adjustable cup tool - $11.50
   a) Uses - adjustable crank bearing cup
   b) Home

16. Lock ring/headset tool $7
    a) Lock ring on adjustable crank bearing cup, raising and lowering headset
    b) Home

17. Swiss Army Knife - Champion model $45
    a) Uses - metal file blade for protruding spoke heads, Phillips screwdriver for small screws holding LeTour generator light lens (has 13 additional blades/features)
    b) Home, commuting, touring

18. Vise grips - $8
    a) Uses - removing blips from wheel rims; hand-vise when needed
    b) Home

19. Crescent wrench 15" - $14
    a) Uses - removing freewheel, cotterless crank
    b) Home

20. Third hand brake tool - $1.50
    a) Uses - adjusting brakes
    b) Home

21. Freewheel sprocket tools - two, $6.95 pair
    a) Uses - changing freewheel sprockets
    b) Home

The following items are not tools *per se*, but should be listed here because of their association with repair work at home.

1. Bike tuning stand - Persons $4.50; Sun Tour $9.50

a) Uses - lifts rear wheel off the ground for adjusting derailleurs, chain, crank arms
b) Home

2. Floor pump with air gauge - $15
   a) Uses - quicker, more convenient than the hand-held pump carried on the road; the built-in air gauge is priceless - no need to let air out while checking pressure with hand gauge
   b) Home

3. Ball bearing grease - there are several different kinds available, and all come in a tube except for the kind I now use exclusively at home - Drydene #4000. This comes in a plastic tub, and includes a syringe applicator. I have found that it withstands rain and heat very well, and enduring even beyond 3,000 miles worth of travelling. It costs about $4 per pound, compared with $1.50 for a 3-ounce tube of Phil Wood grease. Bike catalogues do not carry this Drydene Lube, but you can send to this address for it:

   JR Touring Cycles
   P.O. Box 34127
   Bethesda, MD 20034

4. Oil - again, several different kinds are available. Two which I have used and liked are:
   Sturmey Archer, 8.8 ounce can - $2.50
   Cycle Pro, 7 ounce can - $1.30

5. Wheel truing stand - Although I depend upon my thumbs and eyes for perfect align-

ment, Palo Alto catalogue has a stand which appears quite reasonable. $15.

Just a few more words before we go on to repairs. Commuters will be able to get by quite nicely without the Swiss Army Knife mentioned above, though I strongly suggest it for touring. Also, if you aren't working on several bikes, you won't require two of the "universal" tools (numbers 13 and 14) above. I suggest purchasing only those tools necessary for commuting first, and six months to a year later buying those which you'll need for maintenance on wheel hubs and your crank assembly. This way your initial expenditure will be about $45, with another $40 outlay the second time around. I know this sounds steep, but remember what you're buying: a complete set of lifetime tools for about the same cost as one good automobile tire. Now, on to repairs.

BASIC BIKE

2.

No sooner will you get home from the shop with your beautiful new bike than an adjustment of the handlebars and saddle will be required. In fact, you should expect to be making minor adjustments for the first few days on a new machine, until it feels like part of you when you mount up. Therefore, we'll begin with the adjustments of these two parts, and move on from there.

The bike shop salesman has probably told you all about the importance of saddle height. But in case you've forgotten, let me remind you that personal comfort and pedalling efficiency can be attained only by placing the saddle just where it belongs. If the frame has been properly fitted to you then you'll have no trouble putting the saddle in its correct position. But if the frame is too short, you'll have to buy an extra-long seat post. If you fail to do this, and end up leaving your saddle too low, your legs will not be able to stretch as you pedal, and the result will be muscle cramps.

Correct saddle height is that which allows for full extension of the legs during pedal rotation. When the pedal is at the end of its down-stroke (six o'clock position) it should be too low for your instep or heel to reach it - just the ball of your foot must be on the pedal. Toe-clips and straps make this much easier, and also make possible a technique called "ankling" which greatly increases pedal efficiency.

Look closely at your saddle and you'll see that it can be adjusted in four ways - height, tilt, a movement forward or backward to increase or decrease the distance from the saddle nose to handlebar stem (gooseneck), and movement from side to side. Let's run through these separately.

Saddle Adjustment:

1. Height - your saddle sits on top of the seat post, which must be raised or lowered for the adjustment we wish. What holds this seat post in place is the bolt which goes through the frame directly behind the post itself. The bolt head is usually round, with a small metal tip beneath it which fits a frame slot, designed to hold the bolt steady when tightening the nut on the opposite side. Usually, just loosening the nut will not allow the post to move, especially after you've had the bike for a while. To get it to move you'll have to take hold of the saddle and twist it from side to side, pulling up or pushing down at the same time. (I use bike grease or petroleum jelly on my seat post to keep if from freezing or rusting in place.) Once the saddle is at the height you wish, merely tighten the seat post bolt nut, and you're done.

Whereas vise grips, channel locks, or a crescent wrench will all do the job, I suggest you refrain from using the first two mentioned due to their serrated teeth, which leave unsightly hash marks on the nut. Since you'll always have a 6" crescent wrench in your bike bag, you may as well use the correct tool. And a word of caution when using crescents - if you don't buy a good wrench, and if you don't snug the sliding jaw right up to a nut or bolt head, there is a good chance that you'll "round" the corners. Do this a few times and you'll have real trouble getting a hold on the nut. I have a full set of open and box-end metric tools in my basement, and so if at home, I use one of these to insure an even greater fit around the seat post nut. On the road, however, the crescent is my choice. *

2. Tilt - each rider finds a particular slant of the saddle preferable to him, if of course he knows that such a choice is available. To produce this angle you will need, on most saddles, two wrenches; any of the three mentioned above are acceptable, though I prefer a vise grips and a 6" crescent. The saddle underside has two long metal bars which run nearly the length of the seat, and which are wider toward the rear, narrower toward the front or nose of the saddle. Attached to these bars is a double clamp with a hole in the center for the seatpost, and a single metal bar threaded on both ends. This bar runs through the two clamps and has a nut on either end. Tighten the nut and the clamps tighten upon the long metal bars beneath the seat, while also narrowing the center hole and thereby securing the saddle to the seat post.

While the saddle is on the bike, place one

---

* Many seatpost bolts now have allen head nuts on either side, requiring allen wrenches of the proper size in place of crescents or channel locks.

wrench on one clamp nut, holding it fast. (This is why I prefer the vise grips, for it holds by itself and frees my hand.) With the second wrench loosen the second clamp nut until it moves freely; then, apply force to the saddle rear or nose to move it into place. Finally, tighten the clamp nut securely. If you look closely at the clamps you will notice grooves or serrated edges on the clamp faces, to help hold the saddle in place. When you tighten the clamp nuts make sure the grooves are matched properly.

3. Forward and backward movement - this adjustment facilitates riders who, while taking the same size bike due to leg length, have arms of different length. Different sized handlebars are available for this purpose. Additionally, you can tilt the handlebars up a bit to allow for easy reach of the brake hoods. The saddle is also designed to aid in this fitting.

To slide the saddle forward or backward merely loosen the clamp nuts as in "2" above, position the seat where you wish, and tighten the nuts again.

4. Side-to-side movement - the nose of the saddle should point directly forward over the bicycle top tube, but sometimes will be cocked to one side or the other if the seat post bolt has worked loose. To straighten this you should, as in "1" above, loosen the seat post bolt nut, position the saddle correctly, and tighten.

Note: Some bicycles with center-pull brakes have a metal bracket attached to the seat post bolt, and movement of the nut on this bolt can tighten the brake cable by tilting the bracket up. I usually place the flat side of a crescent wrench across the metal bracket and gently push it back into position.

Note: Some fancy saddles have attachment systems other than the clamp-type just described. One such model has two bolts pointing downward from beneath the saddle, therefore making it quite difficult to reach the bolt head with a regular wrench. Special wrenches are available for this purpose, which are bent like a flattened S, but I would never commute or tour with the extra weight.

Two types of saddle attachment.

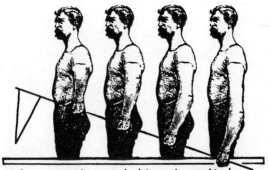

The saddle and the handlebars
adjust to facilitate riders with
arms of different length.

3.

Problems with handlebars usually fall into one of the following categories:

1. loose bars
2. loose brake lever
3. need for new bar tape
4. bars difficult to turn from side to side
5. need to raise or lower bars.

(All directions will refer to the popular "drop-bars" found on most bikes today. These are the bars which curl forward and downward like a ram's horns.)

1. Loose bars - handlebars can be loose in two ways: they can slip upward or downward, and they can slip from side to side while your wheel is still heading straight down the road. With bars slipping up or down, the remedy is to tighten the handlebar binder bolt, located in the middle of

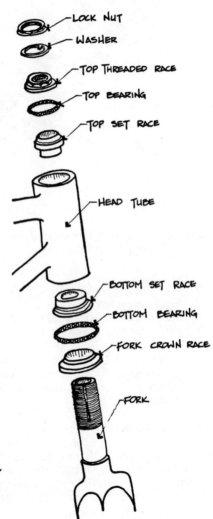

LOCK NUT

WASHER

TOP THREADED RACE

TOP BEARING

TOP SET RACE

HEAD TUBE

BOTTOM SET RACE

BOTTOM BEARING

FORK CROWN RACE

FORK

HEADSET

the bar and at the end of the stem. Most bikes require a small crescent wrench for this adjustment, but some have an allen head. (Allen wrenches of the correct size only should be used; sometimes a smaller-size allen can be made to turn the bolt by using the wrench at an angle. However, this wears down the inside of the bolt head, and therefore should be avoided.)

Bar slippage from side to side (while the wheel remains straight) requires a tightening of the handlebar expander bolt, the head of which rests on the top of the stem or "gooseneck". By tightening this bolt the "wedge nut" is pulled up inside the stem, thereby expanding the stem wall against the head tube, and locking it into place. (A second popular style of expander bolt system is the angled expander, which works in the same way.) When making this adjustment I straddle the front wheel, facing the bicycle, placing my knees on either side of the fork. When I am sure I have the bar positioned properly I tighten the expander bolt.

2. Loose brake lever - if you ride a great deal with your hands on the brake hoods your brakes will, after a long while, slip downward on the bar. To remedy this you will have first to trigger your brake release (if you have one) or, remove the brake cable from the brake, or remove the brake pads. (For clarification see the section on brake repair.) This is necessary in order to fully depress the brake lever on the bar, thereby exposing the apparatus which holds the brake hand lever on the bar. You will see a screw-head directly behind the brake cable; this is what must be tightened to prevent further movement of the lever. If you use a long, thin-shanked screwdriver to turn the screw you won't have to remove the brake cable to make the adjustment.

3. New bar tape - handlebar tape, like all things on these beautifully aesthetic and efficient machines, makes the bike look complete, and performs a necessary function. That multiple function is: *a)* to allow for a good, fast grip on the bar, *b)* to absorb perspiration from the hands, and *c)* to cushion you from road shock. Cloth and leather tape provide for all these needs; plastic tape, however, has only its bright color going for it and represents a Detroit inroad into biking which will be stamped out once riders understand the form and function of their mounts. Tape should be added when old tape wears out; when I used cloth tape I always wound new over the old, both for greater absorption and so that I might have a thicker bar to hold with my large hands. During the last eighteen months I have used all-leather tape, which I find the best yet. I oil it just as I do my leather toe clips and straps and saddle, and it has held up beautifully (Bike Warehouse, $8.50).

Replacing tape is not difficult, though it requires a bit of practice. I always begin at the top of the bar next to the stem, with two or three wrappings laid over one another. Next, I begin by angling across the bar, overlapping each winding with approximately one-third of the next. I do not remove the brake hand-lever or brake hood for taping, but merely wrap around it. The tricky point is ending up with the right amount of tape at the end of the bar. This tape end will be secured in place by removing the bar and plug, stuffing the tape inside, and replacing the plug securely (which often requires a sharp rap or two with a mallet or hammer or heel of the hand). There is no problem with having a good deal of extra tape left over, for you will just cut off the excess, leaving the necessary two or three inches to push into the bar and hole. (But first check your windings; tape manufacturers know exactly what length is required, and I have never wound up with an excess.) If you are short by a few inches, which invariably happens the first time or two, just rewind carefully, overlapping a tiny bit less each time.

4. Bars difficult to turn from side to side - this problem, though at first glance a handlebar-related difficulty, is actually the fault of the headset. The headset secures the fork to the frame, but must also allow for free movement of the fork to either side. The diagram of the headset and fork will show how this dual purpose is made possible; the top tube of the fork is threaded, and held in place in the head tube by the top threaded race (bearing cup). This race, and the fork crown race, are positioned with the top and bottom bearings to allow for rotation. In all my riding the greatest difficulty I've had with headsets was remedied in a fifteen minute repair: first, using a large crescent (10" or greater) when home (my small channel locks on the road), I loosen the large lock nut at the top of the headset. Next I loosen the top threaded race, but only slightly, until I can see the bearings inside, but before they can leap out and hide from me on the floor. I then squirt cycle oil into the mass of bearings, very carefully allow the fork to slip down a fraction of an inch to expose the bottom bearings, and add oil there. This being done I tighten the top threaded race, then the lock nut on top, until there is no upward or downward movement within the headset, but free movement of the fork from side to side. (Your top and bottom bearings may be set inside a small metal retainer cup. If so, you stand a smaller chance of losing them; apply oil as indicated.) Now, if you drop some bearings out of the headset, and do not know if they came from the top or bottom races, you'll have to take all the bearings out of both, divide them in half and replace them. If you come up with an odd number of bearings, even after searching everywhere on the floor and your pants cuffs, you have probably lost one. Take a bearing to a bike shop and buy some of the same size.

A word about bearings - whereas headsets are not usually a problem, wheel and crank bearings sometimes need replacing, and not just oil or grease. A bearing should be round and smooth on its surface. Sand and the usual road grime will tend to "pit" bearings, and after a while will flake off a piece of the surface. If these bearings remain in your bike they will wear upon axles and races until they too will require replacement. Bearings are extremely inexpensive compared to these parts. So don't forget the axiom about an ounce of prevention.

5. Raising and lowering the bars - this procedure gives many riders fits, for they don't understand what you already know about expander bolts and wedge nuts (reread "1" above). Usually a rider will loosen the expander bolt completely, then straddle the front wheel and tug at the bar for all he's worth. The problem is that the wedge nut is still frozen in place. To remedy this, the expander bolt must be rethreaded a few turns, and a sharp rap with a mallet delivered to the top of the expander bolt. This will free the wedge nut, and by turning the handlebars while pulling up or pushing down at the same time, you will be able to raise or lower your bars.

Note: always leave 2" to 2 1/2" of stem in the headset for a proper and safe grip.

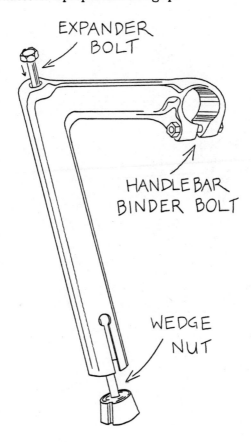

EXPANDER BOLT

HANDLEBAR BINDER BOLT

WEDGE NUT

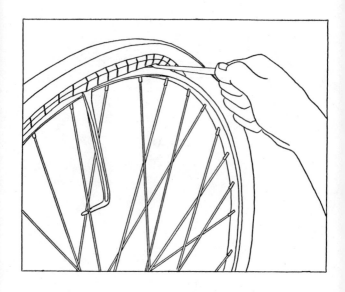

4.

We'll discuss wheels in the following problem categories:

1. flats ("punctures" to the British)
2. wheel alignment
3. broken spokes
4. bearing maintenance
5. freewheel removal

1. Flats -The tools necessary for this repair are:
   a) Tire levers -small metal levers used to pry the tire bead from its seat in the rim. You only need two, but of course most manufacturers sell them in lots of three, for about $1. The levers should be steel, not aluminum (more weight, I know, but the lighter ones always bend on me), and should have a hole cut away on one side so as to hold onto the spokes. Also, if your shop or bike catalogue has levers of two different lengths choose the longer ones, for they'll be far easier to use and thereby justify the additional weight.

b) 6" crescent wrench - to remove the wheel axle nuts, unless you have quick-release wheels.

c) Tube patch kit or new tube - the patch kit costs about 50 cents, has a tube "rougher" (to make the rubber more adhesive), glue, and patches of different sizes.

A word of warning. This very simple repair can be troublesome until you've done it a few times - like learning to tie your shoe laces. So don't complicate matters by substituting screwdrivers for tire levers. Screwdrivers were designed for screws, and will only put holes in your tubes and rips in your tire if you use them in place of the correct tool. Even on my world ride, when I pared every imaginable bit of weight from my touring load, I still carried tire levers. And now back to fixing a flat. (Steps "A" through "K".)

a) You must begin by removing the wheel from the frame. Let's deal with the front wheel first, since it's considerably easier. You will recall that I spoke earlier of releasing the brakes, in the section on handlebars. This release is necessary because of the width of the tire being somewhat greater than the space between the brake pads. Most expensive brake sets have a quick-release mechanism operable with the flick of a finger. I didn't have this convenient option until a year ago, and therefore merely used a crescent wrench to take off one of the brake pads. (See section on brake repair.) Some riders prefer to remove the cable, by squeezing the two brake pads together on a centerpull brake and slipping off the cable carrier, or the barrel cable end. Whichever you prefer, once the brake pads are out of the way you may move to the next step.

b) Release the wheel, either by tripping the quick-release on the hub, or loosening the axle nuts.

c) Pull the wheel away from the frame. This may require a degree of effort, for the fork blades are sometimes machined so as to be actually narrower than the axle. Also, study the dropouts so that you will be pulling the wheel in the correct direction.

Note: I do all this while my bike is on its back, for this is the way I do it on the road. Some riders suggest the use of a bike rack at home, and prefer to lay the bike on its side (never the derailleur side) when on the road, rather than upside down. Their reasoning is sound, for putting a bike on its back will, in time, crack the cable housing coming out of the hand brake levers. However, spoke replacement and wheel alignment require the bike to be upside down, so I merely place a couple turns of electricians' tape on the cracked housing, and forget about it.

d) If your rear tire is flat (and more than 90% of all my flats have been in back), you'll have more difficulty in removing the wheel. First, trip your quick-release brake lever or remove one brake pad. Then shift the chain into the smallest sprocket on the cluster. (It does not matter which sprocket in front holds the chain.) Next, trip your axle quick-release, or loosen the axle nuts. Holding the wheel with your right hand, reach to the rear derailleur housing with your left, and take hold of the body. Gently, pull the derailleur up and back toward yourself. This will move the chain out of the way of your small sprocket, and the wheel can be removed.

e) Remove the tire and tube from the wheel.

This is accomplished with the aid of your tire spoons. Take the lesser-angled end of one tire spoon and, beveled-end up, work it underneath the tire bead about a half-inch. Now push downward on the tire lever end in your hand - that is - toward the spokes. Hook the slotted side onto a spoke to hold the tire in place. (This frees both your hands for the rest of the work.) Take a second lever and, once again, work the tip underneath the tire bead, about 1" from the first lever. Again, push downward on your lever, to pop the bead away from its seat in the rim. If you can't do this, move your lever a half-inch closer to the first lever. Now continue to work the bead away from the rim all around the wheel, until you have one complete side of the tire off the rim. Then, using your spoon from the opposite side of the wheel, work the second bead off the rim. (You are now working the bead off the rim-side away from you, as of course both beads must come off the same side to free the tire.) Taking one side of the tire off at a time is much easier than trying to force both beads off at once.

Note: when you begin working with the first tire lever be sure to start at a point on the wheel opposite to or at least away from the valve stem. Also, new tires are difficult to remove the first time, so be prepared to spend some time.

f) Take the tube out of the tire, and check the outside and inside of the tire for embedded glass, pebbles, thorns, etcetera. When you are sure that it is clear, move on to the tube. I have had only two holes in my life which leaked so little that I was forced to hold them under water to look for air bubbles. All the other times I merely pumped up the tube and listened for escaping air. (Once, I heard air coming out of the center of the valve. If you look at a tube valve carefully you will see that the inside is threaded. If this core is not screwed into place tightly it will result in a leak. The proper tool to tighten a valve core is the valve cover tool, a tiny slotted metal cap which you should buy to replace the worthless black plastic caps present on all the tubes sold. If you have a very slow leak check that your valve core is tight before you remove the wheel from the frame.)

g) Once the hole is located you can rough up the area with the patch kit scraper. Be sure to do a good job of it, short of putting additional holes in the tube, and be sure to roughen an area a bit larger than the size of the patch.

h) Apply the glue, again a bit more than necessary to cover the patch area. Most kits suggest waiting until the glue is dry to apply the patch. So, wait. Hurry this step and there's a good chance you'll be taking the wheel back off the bike a few miles down the road. Be careful not to touch the patch side which goes on the tube, and once in place press the edges of the patch with a tire spoon.

i) If you have done all things properly thus far you can reassemble the wheel immediately, and ride on. But, before you do, check that the "tape" is in place. This is usually the black rubber or cloth wrapping which sits on the rim, covering the spoke ends. If you remove the tape you can see spoke nipple ends; spokes of the wrong length would protrude through the tape and into the tube. Spokes of correct length, when adjusted for alignment, or, just by the normal tension produced when riding, sometimes twist up past the nipple top. The tape protects the tube from the resultant punctures. Replacement tapes, if you break one, are available at bike shops or from catalogues. I have used a piece of scotch tape and even a staple in the past for repair, and gauze as replacement one time on tour.

j) Pump up the tube slightly, so that it can easily be placed inside the tire, without fear of wrinkles in the rubber. Once the tube is replaced, push the valve stem through the hole in the rim, making sure that it is completely pushed through, and that it *remains* perfectly perpendicular to the rim at all times. Riders who fail to do this, or who ride with low air pressure in their tires (which causes the tube to shift and the valve stem to angle out of the hole), cause wearing of the stem along its side and base. Once a hole occurs in the valve stem the entire tube is shot, for stems cannot hold a patch.

With the stem in place, begin putting one side of the tire back on the rim. (At this point, when working with PR puncture-resistant tubes, I release the air inside. It makes replacement easier.) When taking the tire off you began at a point opposite the stem; when replacing a tire you begin at the valve stem. You should be able to put one side of the tire back on the rim by hand alone, without spoons, though a new tire or inexperience may require their use. Once one side is fully in place, and again starting at the valve, tuck the other bead into its home in the rim.

You will end up with six inches or so of tire which seems to be far too short to stretch into place. But remember that the tire was on the same rim before, and that the name for this type of tire - clincher - is given for its ability to "clinch" itself to the wheel. Use your spoon in the opposite manner to replace the tire, and use it with beveled-end down. If both beads are properly seated, and the stem is still perpendicular, inflate the tire to its desired pressure. Do this before you put the wheel back on the bike, for it will mean less to mess with if you have goofed with the patch. But don't worry. A chimp can master a patch kit.

k) If the tire remains hard for a minute slap it back on your bike and pedal off. *But, do not forget to reset your brakes.*

2. Wheel alignment - "truing" your wheels is an adjustment most successfully done with a stand made especially for this purpose. I must admit to not owning one, and never having owned one. In fact, I took my first cross-country ride without even knowing a wheel could come out of true. When I first had to align a badly battered wheel it was on the road, and of course without a truing stand within a hundred miles. And all the times since then when I've had to align my wheels it has been while on the road, on tour. So, I'll teach you my method, the one which will get you back home if you break down.

Wheels can be out of true in two ways: they can sway from side to side, and they can have high and low spots - which is referred to as being out of "round". Look closely at your wheel. Notice that the spokes reach out to the rim from both sides of the hub. Focus upon one spoke and think what tightening (shortening the length of) that single spoke will do. It should be obvious to you, if you are really thinking, that the rim will be pulled in two directions at the same time when the spoke is tightened, or moved back in two directions if loosened. Tighten the spoke and the rim will be *1)* pulled closer to the hub, and *2)* pulled in the direction of the side of the hub to which the other end of the spoke is attached. Loosen the spoke and the opposite movement will occur. Tighten a spoke which comes from the other side of the hub and the rim will move in that direction. As you can see the spokes must be equal in tension to produce a "straight" or a "true" wheel.

You may wonder why spokes ever come out of alignment. Ponder for a moment what the job of the unappreciated spoke is - and the enormous tension it is placed under. They are the most slender, delicate parts of your machine, yet they are the major instrument of support for your body, all your gear, and the rest of the bike. Not only must they hold you up, and fly around and around at tremendous speeds, but they must balance you when you are wheeling around a tight curve at a 45 degree angle to the ground. Ever wonder why you don't fall over when you're doing that? Try keeping your feet pressed together; have a friend tilt you at a 45 degree angle, and see if you are still standing a second after he or she lets go. The reason a bike doesn't fall is the revolving wheels - the gyroscopic action applied when riding.

Now that you appreciate the spokes a bit more, let's get on to adjusting them. If you study a new wheel closely, running your hand along the spokes, you'll notice that they all appear to have the same amount of tension. Of course, that seems logical when you think of the need for the wheel to be held just as tightly by the spokes coming from one side of the hub as from the other, so that the wheel will be straight. If you were to break one spoke, or loosen one greatly, the wheel would be pulled harder to that side of the hub which still has all its spokes at proper tension. It's like a tug-of-war, with two sides pulling at a rope. When one side weakens, the rope (or rim) is pulled to the stronger side.

Normal riding over city streets will, in time, knock any spoked wheel out of true. How much time? Well, this depends upon your weight, road conditions, kind of spoke and hub, amount of "dishing" (the degree to which the spokes on the right side of the rear wheel are "flattened" to allow for the cluster space on the axle), and several other factors. When I'm on tour and carrying heavy loads I check my wheel alignment at least once a week. At home, I'm ashamed to say that usually I feel the sway of a misaligned wheel before I remember to check it. (Sort of like motorists neglecting the water level in the battery, until the winter morning when the engine won't turn over.) If I failed to correct the wobble, I would in time snap a spoke, so let's deal with the small wobbles first.

I have yet to align a wheel by adjusting just one spoke. Generally, five or so must be worked with - and sometimes more. My method of truing is the following:

a) Take your tire, tube and tape off the wheel. (This allows for a more accurate truing, and exposes the screw head of the spoke nipple for adjustment with a screwdriver. It also allows you to *see* if too much spoke extends through the nipple head - a real danger to your tube.)

b) Place the wheel back on the bike. (Your bike is of course on its back.)

c) Spin the wheel with your hand, noting the wobble side-to-side.

d) To determine the extent of the wobble, place your thumb next to the wheel rim (with the palm of your hand resting on the chainstay bar) so that your thumbnail lightly touches the rim at every point except for the wobble. At that point the rim will reach out and smack your thumbnail - your job is to pull that wobble back into line with the rest of the rim.

e) Check the tension of the spokes in the area of the wobble. Chances are they'll be a bit more loose than the rest of the spokes in the wheel. Usually I am most successful in tightening the spoke at the center of the wobble, and least successful tightening for the other spokes as we move farther from the worst wobble point.

f) But how do you tighten a spoke? And what if two spokes appear to sit right smack in the middle of the problem area? Easy - just recall that spokes reach out to the rim from both sides of the hub. Naturally, tightening a spoke coming from the right side pulls the rim toward the right; from the left hub side, to the left. If your wobble is to the right, you'll be tightening the spokes in that area of the rim which come from the left side of your hub. (I prefer to use a small screwdriver in the nipple slot head - and I always start off with a slight adjustment, about a half-turn for the spoke at wobble center, 1/4 turn for spokes on either side, 1/8 turn for the next two spokes. You can also tighten spokes with a "spoke nipple wrench", but the flat sides on these nipples tend to round-off quickly. Therefore, I only use the spoke nipple wrench when I am adjusting spokes with the tire still on the rim - something I only do in an emergency.)

g) On occasion you might have to loosen some spokes and tighten some others in the wobble area to produce a true wheel, especially if you have trued your wheel several times before. In loosening spokes, follow the same pattern as above, more toward wobble center, less thereafter.

h) When your thumbnail-guide tells you all is well, you have two final things to do. First, check your spokes for approximately the same tension on all. You won't be perfect on this, but at least be close, or you'll be aligning your wheel again real soon. Secondly, step to the side of your bike, spin the wheel and check for its "round". If you have one high spot tighten the spokes slightly in this area - to pull the rim toward the hub a bit. But be sure to watch that you don't lose your side-to-side true as you do this.

i) I would like to add, as a postscript to wheel alignment, that this has got to be the most exasperating repair work on a bike. Take it easy, and keep your cool. Losing your temper will not force those spokes into place.

Bikers use the terms "wobble" and "blip" to denote different problems. "Wobble" is corrected by spoke adjustment, as you have just learned. But "blip" refers to a bulge in the rim, a condition which no amount of spoke alignment will eradicate. This problem usually results from riding with tires woefully underinflated, or from riding into huge potholes, sewer drains, trying to jump curbs, and so on. Luckily, I've never had a bad blip on my wheels (though I've dealt with more than my rightful share of broken spokes and wheel wobbles). However, on a rough ride through downtown St. Louis my cycling companion once produced a real beauty on his rear wheel. Due to its size he was unable to keep his rear brakes applied when he needed to, for the brake pads touch on the very part of the rim where blips appear. We stopped at a service station to borrow a pair of vise-grips, and cut two thin shims of wood from an old paint can stir-stick. We placed these pieces next to the rim, inside the vise-grip jaws, then squeezed very carefully. This did the trick for us, but if you someday have a blip which remains on one side of the rim after the other side has been restored, or if a blip has appeared on only one side to begin with, place the wood shim on the flat side, and have a go at the fat blip with the metal jaw of the vise grip. But, squeeze gently, and watch both sides of the rim so that you do not push it past its proper profile.

3. Broken spokes - spokes need to be replaced when *1)* they snap when you are riding, and *2)* when the nipple heads are frozen in place on the spoke threads, refusing adjustment. In this second instance you'll just have to use the diagonal clipper portion of your needle-nose pliers to snap the spoke, and buy a new one.

You already know how to align your wheel, so don't let spoke replacement scare you. That is, unless you are in the middle of Hungary when you hear that terrible "snap" in your rear wheel, see that you've lost a spoke on the freewheel side, and then recall that you don't have a freewheel puller in your tool bag. But we'll fix you up so you'll never be in that position.

Look closely at your hub and you will see that the spokes enter the spoke holes in an alternating pattern - every other spoke head will be visible when you view your hub from one side. Let's imagine you have neglected your wobbly rear wheel for so long that a spoke snaps on your way home from work. We'll go in steps through the repair process.

a) Get your cursing over as soon as possible - before you start the repair.

b) Stop riding your bike and fix it, for riding with one broken spoke soon causes a second break, and so on.

c) Remove your panniers, take out your tools and one of the extra spokes you carry at all times taped behind your seat tube - then flip your bike on its back.

d) Take off your rear wheel, remove the tire, tube, and rim tape. If the break is on the free-wheel side, remove the freewheel (see "freewheel removal" below).

e) Remove the broken spoke. This is very easy, for spokes break at the bevel, and can then be taken out by pulling from the nipple end.

f) Take the nipple from the new spoke. Look at the rear hub, and concentrate on the next closest spokes to the one that broke. If you see two spoke heads next to the empty hole in the hub you know that your new spoke must enter from the other side, to follow the alternating pattern around the entire hub. Guide the spoke into the hole. (Don't be afraid to bend the spoke a bit.) Once it is completely through, look at the next closest spoke which enters the hub in the same direction as your replacement spoke. This will be your guide on lacing your replacement - how many spokes you must cross, and which to go over or under with the new spoke. (You'll have to bend the spoke even more here - be sure to bend it along its entire length, thereby not putting a crimp in it.)

g) Put the nipple into the rim, and thread the new spoke into it. Tighten the spoke until it is approximately the same tension as the rest, then align the wheel.

h) Check to see that the new spoke shaft does not protrude past the nipple. If it does, use the metal file of your Swiss Army Knife (a constant companion in your tool bag) to file it down.

i) Replace rim tape, tube, tire; inflate, and ride on.

j) Realize that if you looked after your alignment once in a while you wouldn't have broken the spoke to begin with.

4. Wheel bearing maintenance - bearing maintenance on a bike - cleaning and lubricating old bearings, or replacing them if necessary - is a procedure which I go through twice a year (more often if my touring takes me along many dirt roads). The entire operation, including the bearings in the crankset, takes about two hours. And for this investment of time I have a machine which rolls beautifully and pedals easily. As with all mechanical directions the operation seems impossibly difficult at first. But stay with it, master the only difficult part of cone adjustment, and you'll be one step further toward independence on the road. We'll begin with front wheel bearings.

a) As you can see in the diagram, a front wheel hub consists of a hub shell, two sets of bearings, two dust caps, an axle, two cones, two keyed lockwashers, and two lock nuts. (Add to this your quick-release mechanism, or large axle nuts and washers which hold the wheel on the frame.)

b) Remove the front wheel from the bike, and take off the frame-mounting axle nuts and washers, or the quick-release. (The latter may be removed by holding the handle side fast, while unscrewing the other "bale-nut" end. Notice the

two cone-shaped springs which are held in place
on the axle by the handle and bale-nut - be sure
to replace them later in the same direction as
they were originally, with smaller end toward
hub, larger toward fork blade.)

c) Holding the locknut on one side of the hub
with a crescent wrench, use a second wrench to
loosen the locknut on the opposite hub side.
Unscrew the locknut completely, putting it
somewhere so that you'll not kick it as you continue working. Next remove the keyed lockwasher. (The term "keyed" is used to denote the
small pointed flange of metal on the inside of the
washer - which fits into the groove on the axle.)

REAR HUB

d) You are now to the cone, the piece named for its tapering end which rests against the bearings. To adjust the amount of pressure placed on the bearings by this cone the other end of the cone is squared for a "cone wrench" - a very thin wrench which should be used for no other mechanical purpose than that for which it was designed. (It will last you a life time if you treat it right - just like your bike.) Take hold of the squared-off end with the cone wrench and back it off the axle completely.

e) When this is done you have freed one side of the axle, and are free to pull the other axle side out of the hub. Do so, watching for small bearings which might fall out.

f) Now, take a small screwdriver and place the flat edge beneath the dust cap on the hub. This cap is designed to hold the bearings in place, and to fit so snugly into the hub as to keep out water and dirt. Therefore, it will be difficult to remove, and you may have to lift the cap in several places with the screwdriver before it comes out.

g) With the dust cap gone, look at your bearings. If you are pulling frequent maintenance there will be grease covering them still; this is a good sign that you have not waited so long that damage to your components might have occured. Count the bearings, and notice, before you remove them, the small space present - bearings are not supposed to be wedged tightly into place. Now remove the bearings, cleaning and inspecting each individually for pitting or cracks. Bearings cost about 70 cents for a bag of twenty or more; a single hub costs from $20 on up. If you save a few cents by keeping cracked or pitted bearings you'll lose dollars in the end with a pitted hub. So replace them when they need it.

(Be sure to buy a bag of each size bearing you might need before you break down your wheel. Otherwise you'll be walking to the bike shop.) Bearing sizes generally fall into the following categories:

      3/16" - front hubs

      1/4"- rear hubs, bottom brackets

      1/8" - freewheel

      5/32" - pedals, headsets

h) Once both dust caps and all bearings are removed and cleaned, take out the grease remaining in the hub, and wipe it clean with a cloth. Do the same to the underside of each dust cap. You are now ready to rebuild your wheel.

i) Apply a bead of fresh grease to the bearing cup of one side of your hub. Replace the bearings; then cover them with a second liberal bead of grease. Replace the dust cover by tapping it lightly with a small tack hammer, though any tool with a bit of weight and a flat side will do - when on the road I use the 6" crescent wrench.

j) Take the axle (which still has the cone, lockwasher and locknut on one side) and insert it into the hub side in which you have just replaced the bearings. Be sure to have cleaned and checked the cones - for they too are far less expensive to replace than an entire hub. Now you can turn your wheel over and replace the bearings in the other side, for the dust cap and cone will keep the bearings from falling out.

k) Once the bearings are in place around the axle on this second side, replace the dust cap, thread the cone finger-tight against the bearings, slide on the lockwasher, and screw on the locknut. Your hub is now rebuilt, but not ready to be ridden, for the cones have not been adjusted to the proper pressure against the bearings. Too loose, and the wheels will roll from side to side, in time ruining your bearings and cup and cone. Too tight, and the wheel will not roll properly.

l) Use the cone wrench to back off the cones a quarter turn or less if, when you turn the axle, it does not revolve easily in the hub. (The wheel is still off the bike.) What usually happens is that a person will back off the cones too far, creating side-play. This is when the axle moves back and forth in the hub. Even a slight amount of movement will be greatly accentuated when the wheel is replaced on the frame, so try to remove the side-play while still retaining free rolling movement of the axle. Just when you think you've got the best of both worlds, tighten the locknuts on both sides. (Hold one side fast with a crescent wrench or in a vise while tightening the other side.) The first time you do this you will notice that you have tightened the cone against the bearings somewhat by snugging the locknuts - and you'll have to readjust the cone once more. But don't get angry. Merely hold the locknut on one side of the axle fast with your crescent wrench, while backing off the same side cone ever so slightly with your cone wrench. This is usually sufficient for me to align it properly; but if not perfect, just back off the locknut a quarter-turn and try again. Expect it to be difficult at first, and much easier the second time.

m) Once side-play is absent and the axle moves freely, replace the quick-release or axle washers and nuts, and restore the wheel to the frame. Once it is secured, spin the wheel and check again for rolling ease and for side-play. If it is not correct do not sell your bicycle. Go upstairs or into the house, yell or kick the dog, and then return to your bike and adjust your cones once more. But don't give up, and above all do not ride it if you still have side-play.

5. Freewheel removal - the only difference in bearing maintenance for the front and rear wheels is the need to remove the freewheel. Do so by following these steps:

a) When you purchase your bike ask the shop owner which type of freewheel you have - Sun Tour, Shimano, Regina, etcetera. Buy the proper freewheel removal tool (less expensive in bike catalogues - Sun Tour $4, Shimano $4.80, Regina $5.90), for it will always ride with you in your tool bag.

b) Once you have the proper tool, and when you must remove the freewheel to replace a broken spoke on the cluster side, or wish to pull maintenance on your rear wheel bearings, remove the wheel from your bike and take off the axle nuts and washers (or quick-release mechanism). Look inside your freewheel. You will see either splines or two notches. Slip the freewheel tool onto the axle and see if it will engage the splines or notches on the tool securely. If not, and if you have the proper tool, the problem is the presence of a "threaded spacer" blocking your tool's descent into the freewheel. Screw off this spacer from the axle.

c) If you have access to a vise you are well off, for this is the easiest method I know of. You would do well to invest in a pocket vise. It is a 2 ounce device that will allow you a better chance for roadside repair if you have a Sun Tour freewheel, freewheel removal tool, and quick-release hubs ($6, Cycle Sports, P.O. Box 18937, Seattle, WA 98118).

Take the freewheel tool and clamp it tightly in

the vise. (You will see one flattened side for this purpose.) Next, set your wheel on the tool, making sure the splines or notches engage properly. When engaged, take hold of the wheel at the 3 and 9 o'clock positions from where you stand, and turn the wheel counter-clockwise. This will be difficult, especially if you are a strong rider. Once the freewheel gives way you can continue the counter-clockwise movement until you feel the wheel separate from the freewheel; or lift the wheel from the vise and finish unscrewing the freewheel by hand.

What do you do if no vise is around? If at home, or in the vicinity of a service station, you can use what I purchased some time ago and have removed dozens of freewheels with - a 15" crescent wrench. (Once, under duress, I used a large pipe wrench, but I don't suggest it.) Place the removal tool in the crescent's jaws as tightly as possible. Stand over your wheel, the freewheel on the right, your left hand at the top of your rim. Engage the removal tool and freewheel securely, and position the wheel so that the wrench handle angles up toward you, not away from you. Take hold of the wrench and push down on it, being careful not to allow the removal tool to slip out of the freewheel. With the application of a good deal of pressure the free-wheel will "break", and then you can easily thread it off the wheel.

Finally, what do you do if you aren't near a vise or a large crescent or pipe wrench, when a spoke on the freewheel side snaps? For this terrible situation I carry a small channel-locks wrench, only 6 3/4" long overall. This I use in the same manner as the 15" crescent, though with some modification. First, in order to hold the freewheel tool securely in the jaws of the the channel-locks I use a shock cord wrapped around the handles of the wrench. Next I fold a piece of cloth (bandana, sock, T-shirt), over the handle, to save my palm once I begin applying the great force necessary to remove the freewheel with such a small tool. And then I follow the steps described above with the crescent.*

d) When the freewheel is off, you may find a metal or clear plastic "spoke protector" ready to fall off as well. (This is held in place only by the freewheel.) The purpose of this disc is implied by the name; it guards the spokes from the chain if you greatly overshift into your largest sprocket in the rear. Personally, I do not like the looks of the disc, I begrudge the extra weight, and I keep my rear derailleur aligned so as not to worry about such extreme overshifting. I remove my spoke protector disc completely, and do not replace it when rebuilding the wheel.

e) You are now free to pull maintenance on your rear wheel bearings just as you did with the front hub.

---

* The *Pocket Vise* is an ingenious answer for broken spokes on the freewheel side. This dandy two ounce device allows the rider a better chance for roadside repair if he has a Sun Tour freewheel, freewheel removal tool, and quick-release hubs. ($6 Cycle Sports, P.O. Box 18937, Seattle, WA 98118.)

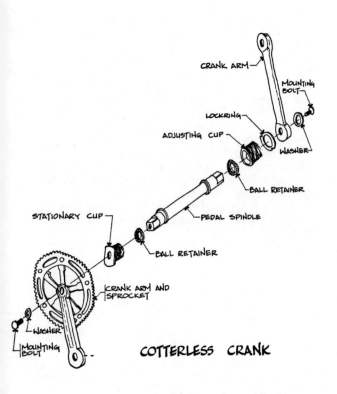

CRANK ARM

MOUNTING BOLT

LOCKRING

ADJUSTING CUP

WASHER

BALL RETAINER

PEDAL SPINDLE

STATIONARY CUP

BALL RETAINER

CRANK ARM AND SPROCKET

WASHER

MOUNTING BOLT

COTTERLESS CRANK

5.

Cotterless - Note in the diagram the various parts of the crank assembly. In our discussion the "right-hand" side will refer to the chainring side, the "left-hand" side to the crankarm without a chainring. Remove, service, and replace your cotterless crank in the following manner:

a) Read the brand name of your crank assembly, or better yet, ask your bike shop dealer when you buy your bike. Then, in the bike shop or through the bike catalogues, purchase the appropriate crankarm removing tool (small enough for carrying in your tool bag, also good for home use - between $4 and $8), or a "universal" crank tool set for approximately $20 (too heavy to carry on the road). The removing tools consist of a wrench to pull the crankarm fixing (mounting) bolt, and the puller assembly itself. When you have the proper tool you may begin servicing your crank.

b) Remove your crankarm dust caps. This can be done with a screwdriver blade on some, and a small allen wrench with others.

c) Remove the crankarm fixing bolts and washers. Most removal tools have one side which slips around the fixing bolt head, with the other end beveled to accept a large crescent wrench. Two of the removal tools, the Sugino Mighty and the Stronglight, have a small breaker bar to take the place of a crescent wrench.

d) Carefully screw the crankarm puller into the crankarm, making sure that the threads meet perfectly. Use your wrench to snug this puller into place.

e) Now insert the extractor portion of the tool into the puller. At first it will move freely. Stop when it reaches the crank spindle (axle). Use your large crescent wrench to turn the extractor gently, and you will see (if you are working first with the right-hand side) the chainrings begin to slip off the spindle toward you. Lift the chain off the chainring and place it out of the way on the spindle housing. Remove the left-hand crankarm in the same way.

f) Look closely at both sides of your crank spindle. The right-hand side is held by a "fixed" bearing cup which is squared-off to accept the large crescent wrench for removal. The left-hand side has an "adjustable" cup which must be removed with either an adjustable cup tool ($8 - $12) or a punch and hammer. (In a bind on tour you can use the edge of a screwdriver as a punch, or the leather punch or fish hook disgorger on your Swiss Army Knife.) The fixed cup is merely threaded completely into the bottom bracket; the adjustable cup is what you will adjust in order to once again to apply only the correct pressure against the bearings. The adjustable cup is held in place by a lockring.

g) Use the crescent wrench or a fixed cup tool (approximately $10, usually with a lockring tool on the other end) to remove the fixed cup, but only once you've put something beneath to catch the bearings should they fall out. (If they don't fall out they are probably held in a "ball-retainer" or "bearing-race". This is a small circular metal holder which allows the bearings to revolve freely inside.) Once the fixed cup is removed, take out the spindle. Notice it has one longer side. This side will be replaced later so as to point toward the chainring.

h) You must first remove the lockring before you can take off the adjustable cup. This is most easily accomplished with a lockring tool, which is properly notched to fit the edges of the lockring. On the road I use a screwdriver blade with something similar to a hammer - the palm of my hand, a piece of wood, a large rock. Back the lockring off the cup completely. Then, using your adjustable cup tool or punch and hammer, remove the adjustable cup from the bottom bracket. Clean, inspect, and replace if necessary all the ball bearings. Wipe all surfaces clean.

i) Apply a generous bead of grease on the inside of your fixed bearing cup, replace the bearings, and cover them with a second layer of grease. Now thread this cup back into the frame (right-hand, chainring side), snugging it with your crescent wrench. (To insure easy removal some months in the future, I always rub a bit of lubricant over the threads inside the bottom bracket before replacing the cups.)

j) Lubricate and replace the bearings in the adjustable cup in the same manner, but do not thread the cup into place yet.

k) Take the cleaned spindle, longer side toward the fixed cup, and, from the other side of the bike (left side) carefully guide it through the bracket and fixed cup. If you have applied a good amount of grease, if your aim with the spindle is accurate, and if you have been kind to motorists all week, you won't knock any of the bearings out of place.

l) While holding the spindle end in one hand, pick up the adjustable cup, engage the spindle in the cup hole, and thread it into the frame. Stop threading this cup when it engages the bearings, and check for side-play in the spindle. If it is present, thread the cup a bit further, but not so far as to prohibit the free turning of the spindle.

m) When the adjustment is correct, replace the lockring, then re-check for proper bearing adjustment.

n) Replace both crank arms by slipping them onto the spindle, and tightening the fixing bolts. These must be secured well, and should be checked for tightness once every 40 or 50 miles for the next 200 miles.

o) Re-engage your chain on the chainring, and replace your dust caps.

Cotterpin - If your crankarms are attached with a pin rather than fixing bolts, you have a cotter-pin crank assembly. Such a set-up is far less desirable than the cotterless system, as removal of the pin is often very difficult. Proceed in the following manner:

a) Using a block of wood as support, rotate your crankarm so that it rests with the nutted end of the pin pointing upwards. Use a crescent wrench to back off the nut to the top of the pin, giving you a larger target to hit with a hammer, and protecting the threads. Place the wood support-block close to the head of the pin, hold the pedal with your left hand, and firmly rap the threaded end of the pin with a hammer.

b) Unfortunately, the pin often will fail to move even when under attack. Do not hammer away at it with all your might, as you'll damage your bearings and hub. Instead, heat the crankarm with a propane torch so that the metal will expand from around the pin, and then knock it free with the hammer.

*c)*Remove the second arm in the same manner, and proceed to bearing maintenance as explained above for cotterless cranks.

Note: When replacing the crankarms, be sure to position pins and axle so that the beveled edges align properly. Such alignment is obtained when the pin can be slipped into place easily, and driven home with a few sharp raps. Use the wood support-block when doing this, and finish by securely tightening the nut on the threaded pin-end.

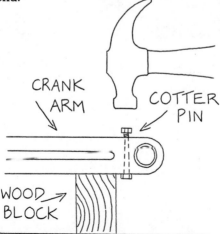

CRANK ARM

COTTER PIN

WOOD BLOCK

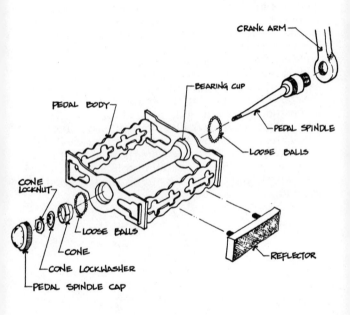

CRANK ARM

BEARING CUP

PEDAL BODY

PEDAL SPINDLE

LOOSE BALLS

CONE
LOCKNUT

LOOSE BALLS

CONE

CONE LOCKWASHER

PEDAL SPINDLE CAP

REFLECTOR

PEDAL

PEDALS

6.

I have never had difficulty with pedals, or
known anyone who did. And, as a result of such
good performance, pedals are often neglected.
They, too, have bearings which should be ser-
viced, and as you can see in the diagram are very
similar to the mechanics of a wheel axle (except
for having a pedal instead of a hub between the
cones). Since the method of servicing is so similar to wheel bearing lubrication, I will be brief.

a) I service my pedals while they are still on
the bike, though you can remove them with a
very thin crescent or open end wrench - thin
enough to fit between the pedal body and the
crank arm. Special pedal wrenches (usually with
a bottom bracket fixed cup remover on the tail
end) are available for $7, but are too heavy for
the road. Once you have a wrench which will fit,
merely back out the pedal spindle from the crank
arm. The left pedal spindle backs out clockwise;
the right is removed counter-clockwise.

b) Remove the pedal dust cap. Some of these caps have serrated edges to allow for easy gripping, but most have an hexagonal head which may be gripped with your crescent or small channellocks, or more easily with a pedal dust cap wrench ($2.25).This handy wrench only weighs an ounce, but is still too heavy for me to ride with, as other tools which I carry will do the job.

c) Remove the locknut and keyed washer, exposing the cone.

d) Due to the pedal housing you cannot get a wrench on the cone; the cone therefore has slots cut in its side (the side facing you) for your screwdriver. Using your small screwdriver blade, back out the cone.

e) Remove the cone, catching all bearings. Slip off the pedal, clean, inspect, and lubricate the bearings, bearing cups and cones.

f) Reassemble. Adjust cone for proper pressure against bearings in the same manner as described in wheel maintenance - free rotation of pedal but no side-play.

7.

Most bikes in the $200 - $300 price range come with the first of the two main types of brakes available:

Center-pulls are named that because the braking action comes from the center - causing the brake pads on either side of the wheel to move together - thus applying pressure on the wheel and slowing its rotation.

Side-pulls are the second main type of brake available. The name again comes from the mechanical action - the brake control cable leading from the handlebars to the brake assembly attaches not at the center but the side.

After worrying about alignment of cones and proper spoke tension, brakes should be relatively simple. One reason is that all parts can be seen readily, and the operation of the brake is easy to understand after just a few minutes of study. You will see the cable leading from the hand brake to one side of the side-pull brake, or to the center of the center-pull. When the hand brake is squeezed, the cable is pulled away from the brake, causing the brakearm or arms to react to the cable tug. The reaction is of course a movement of the brake pads against the wheel rim, which slows the wheel's revolving speed and eventually stops the bike.

You should be able to see the two critical points with brakes. First, the cable must not be so loose as to prohibit a firm pressure against the rim by the brake pads when the brakes are applied and not so tight that the wheel rim is kept from revolving freely when the brakes are not set. Secondly, the brake pads must be in good shape and be positioned so that they strike the rim properly. Aside from an occasional drop of oil on the brake arms when they appear to be sticking (about twice a year), all of my maintenance work on brakes consists of adjusting or replacing the brake cable, and adjusting or replacing brakepads. So let me step you through these repairs.

1. Cable adjustment - almost all good multi-speed bikes today come equipped with an apparatus whereby a brake cable may be lengthened or shortened without the use of a tool - indeed, even while one is riding along. This is facilitated by an "adjusting barrel" of some sort, and is in one of three positions - at the top of the brake arm for side-pull, directly above the center-pull by several inches, or just above the brake hoods on either model. This adjusting barrel or sleeve will shorten a cable when it is turned counter-clockwise, therefore moving the brake pads closer to the rim. There is a locknut or lockring present beneath the barrel which must be loosened to allow the barrel to be moved, and retightened when the adjustment is made to hold the barrel in its new position.

Occasionally, the amount of cable adjustment necessary is beyond that allowed by the adjusting barrel. When this is so, I first screw down the barrel completely, then apply a "third hand" tool ($1.10). This tool fits around the acorn nuts on either brake pad (the nuts on the outside of the pad), holding the pads against the rim to allow much greater ease in changing the cable setting. When on the road I of course do not have this with me, so ask a fellow cyclist to help, or merely do it myself in twice the time. When the tool or friend is in place, or when you are stumbling along by yourself, loosen the anchor bolt which holds the cable in place. (This bolt has a small hole in it, through which the cable runs.) Use your needle nose pliers to pull the cable tight, then tighten your anchor bolt once more. Center-pull brakes have a "carrier" which holds the short transverse cable, and the anchor bolt is located here. Once the brake cable is held fast again by the anchor bolt, release the brake arms. I like the brake pads to rest no further from the rim than necessary to prevent constant rubbing. (This allows for very quick stopping in city riding.) If the brakepads are too close or too far from the rim, re-adjust the cable setting.

2. Cable replacement - someday you'll snap a brake cable, and will be happy that you always have one with you in your bikebag. I prefer to use my little 4" crescent for brake work, though a 6" will suffice. This tool, and the side-cutter portion of your needle nose pliers are all you'll need to replace a brake cable. (Cables run from 60 cents to $1.)

a) Stand in front of your bike and squeeze one of your brake levers. Look inside, and you'll see a screw head. This is what holds the brake lever on the handlebar. (If it becomes loose, use a screwdriver to tighten it.) As you look at the screw head you'll notice your brake cable running in front of it. It is held in place by the barrel or ball end of the cable, which catches the hole or notch inside your brake lever. This hole is designed for either the barrel or ball end, so look to see which type you have by checking out your old cable. Many brake cables come with a barrel on one end, and a ball on the other, so that you will be sure to have the right kind with you at all times. (Bikecology now offers a "pear end" cable which they claim will work in place of both.)

Handbrake. Note brake cable in front of screwhead.

b) Remove the old cable. Cut the end which you don't need off the new cable, and run a few drops of oil over the entire length. Reaching beneath your brake lever, guide the cut end through the barrel or ball slot in the brake lever, then into the plastic cable housing. This will be easier if you have cut the cable so as not to produce a frayed end.

c) When the cable comes out the other end of the housing, guide it through the adjustable sleeve and measure for the proper length by following the steps in brake cable and adjustment above. Secure it with the anchor bolt, and cut off excess cable.

Note - sometimes in winter riding brakes and derailleurs will refuse to work, yet not appear faulty when they are inspected. The problem may well be a frozen cable due to cracked cable housing allowing moisture to enter and freeze up. I spend as little money on my bike as is mechanically wise, and therefore merely tape around small housing cracks. But if it is really battered after several years hard use I do replace it, being careful to cut it without smashing the interior steel casing. Work the diagonal blade of your needlenose in between the wound steel casing so that you are cutting only a single turn of metal. Cost of cable housing runs from 35 cents to $1 per foot.

3. Brake pads - the brake "shoe" includes the metal housing and the pad. One development of late which greatly irritates me is the apparent preference of bike manufacturers to sell one-piece shoes. In other words, when a pad wears out, the metal housing is tossed as well, unlike the two-piece kind which only requires a new pad. This Detroit throw-away mentality is a real motorist intrusion into the more sane world of cycling, and I lament it. So, if you demand two-piece shoes you'll not only save yourself considerable money over the next few decades, but help stop such a waste of machined metal.

Even with my year-round riding in city traffic I find that my brake pads last about ten to twelve months. Pads have a rubber block portion which appears squared off, and a smaller portion which reaches out to the rim. You should replace your pad when it is wearing close to the "block" portion. Be sure to do this earlier if it doesn't seem to be doing its job. Pads by themselves run from 50 cents to $2 apiece. (I use the 50 cent kind.)

In replacing your pads, you must watch out for several things. First, be sure to remount the metal brake shoe so that the closed end is toward the front of the bike. Why? Because the wheels revolve in a forward direction, and will otherwise shoot the pads right out of their metal holders when you squeeze the brakes. Secondly, make sure the pad hits the rim. Some folks say a squeaking brake can be corrected by very gently twisting the brake arm inward with a wrench so that the front of the pad touches the rim first. But I've never done it. All my brake squeaks have been ended by me cleaning my rims of grease and dirt. Most commercial cleaners will work on the rim, as will alcohol, turpentine, kerosene, and gasoline. Just don't get these substances on your tires. They eat rubber.

By the way, the pads will be difficult to take out of the metal shoe. I hold on to the metal stud with my small channel locks or needlenose and place the pad against something immobile.

Then, I push mightily against the open, metal end, and reverse the process to replace them.

Finally, sometimes I find my pads almost black with dirt. When they fail to clean up with alcohol I use the metal file on my Swiss Army Knife, and actually file off 1/16" or so of rubber. It works beautifully, and has kept me from shelling out 50 cents several times over the last decade. Don't laugh. It mounts up - half a buck here and there over the years in biking can soon add up to what it costs a motorist to fill his tank *once*.

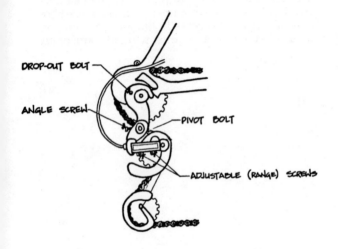

DROP-OUT BOLT

ANGLE SCREW

PIVOT BOLT

ADJUSTABLE (RANGE) SCREWS

REAR DERAILLEUR

DERAILLEURS

8.

Maybe I wouldn't appreciate derailleurs the way I do if I hadn't peered into the workings of a transmission long ago at my auto school. Many of my friends are afraid of their changers, and thus can never be thankful for their beautiful simplicity, and amazing longevity. If you have purchased a moderately good derailleur on a moderately good machine, you'll have to do nothing beyond the simple cleaning, lubricating, and adjusting of your changer to obtain very good performance. And all this can be done without taking your derailleur apart.

I have suggested that anyone with an ability to read thoughtfully and think logically can, if they add a dash of patience, learn to maintain a bike. That goes for derailleurs as well. Look closely at the diagram and at your own bike as you read this. We'll start with the rear derailleur.

Basically, a gear cable runs from your shifters, along your down tube and chain stay, then through a familiar cable adjusting barrel, to a cable anchor bolt on your changer. When you pull back on your shifter lever you tighten the cable, which causes the derailleur to lift the chain from a smaller sprocket, and set it upon a larger one. Naturally, there are limits to how far in either direction you would wish your chain to go, and this limitation is established and maintained by "high" and "low" gear adjusting screws. The high gear screw keeps the chain from moving beyond the smallest sprocket and falling off the freewheel; the low gear screw keeps the chain from moving beyond the largest sprocket and attacking your spokes. The third screw present on some changers is an "angle" screw. Chains, like cables, stretch in time, and thereby change the angle of the derailleur and thus its performance. This angle screw allows for taking up this tiny slack, by resetting the proper angle in relation to the freewheel.

Below the derailleur housing are two pulleys, or rollers. Notice that the chain rolls over one and under the second. The top pulley is the "jockey" pulley - named this for its job of jockeying the chain into place over a sprocket. The bottom one is the "tension" pulley, for it takes up the slack in the chain when the derailleur moves from a larger to a smaller sprocket. And the final thing you should notice - the points of lubrication. Simply apply two drops of oil every month to all springs and moving parts, then wipe off the excess. Now let's run through some very simple procedures which you'll need to follow when problems are encountered.

1. Your bike has fallen over in the mud on the derailleur side, or you haven't cleaned it for eight years now and it won't budge. *The solution:*

a) You are going to have to remove your changer from the bike, and clean it in a pan of some sort of solvent. (I use diesel fuel - a five gallon can of it was forgotten by the previous owners of our house. Kerosene and gasoline also work just fine.) Begin by loosening the cable anchor bolt, and removing the cable.

b) Most derailleurs I see today are affixed to the bike frame with a fork end bracket. One end of this bracket is bolted to the frame with a single bolt and locknut, the other end contains a large hole through which the pivot bolt is secured. (The pivot bolt allows the changer to dance back and forth as you change gears.) And the middle of the bracket is cut away to fit around the axle. You can remove your derailleur by backing out either the single drop-out bolt at the top of the fork end bracket, or the pivot bolt below. (I always remove the drop-out bolt, for unlike the pivot it has only a single locknut to worry about losing.)

c) On many derailleurs the chain will slip off the jockey and tension pulleys without having to disassemble the pulley cage. However, if yours traps the chain between the metal cage sides, remove the pulley spindles with your small crescent wrench. Then slip out the pulley, and allow your chain to hang free.

d) When the cable has been freed from the anchor bolt and adjusting barrel, the drop-out or pivot bolt removed, and the chain freed from the pulley cage, the derailleur is freed from the frame. Swish it about in your solvent, use an old tooth brush to clean the hard-to-reach areas, and pay particular attention to the internal springs if your changer has them.

e) If you have the type pulleys with ball bearings in them remove the cone bushings, clean, inspect, and lubricate the bearings. Reassemble by replacing bearings, threading the cone into the pulley by hand, and adjusting its pressure against the bearings as with all such operations above - free rotation but no side-play. If your pulleys are like mine (without bearings), separate the metal bushing and side plates, clean and oil, and reassemble.

f) Wipe off all solvent from the derailleur, and allow to dry completely.

g) Oil all moving parts and springs, with two drops for the pivot bolt. Re-attach derailleur to bike frame with drop-out or pivot bolt, engage the chain and reassemble pulley cage if necessary. Thread the cable through the cable adjusting barrel and cable anchor bolt. This will be impossible if the cable end is badly frayed; a new cut may be necessary. With chain on smallest rear sprocket and larger front chainring, pull the cable taut with your needlenose pliers, and tighten the cable anchor bolt. Do not pull the cable so taut as to move the derailleur. Also, the adjusting barrel should be screwed down all the way at this point; the barrel adjusts the cable by increasing the distance between the anchor bolt and barrel, and must be twisted counter-clockwise to do so. If the barrel is "up" as far as it will go when the cable is first replaced, it will not be able to adjust the cable at all.

2. Your chain keeps slipping from larger to smaller sprockets. *The solution:*

a) The difficulty is usually located in your shifter assembly, not the derailleur. The shifters become lose after a while and need to be tightened. Remember the difficult job they have they are under constant tension from the cable: they must be able to move easily in your hand when you shift gears, and yet must remain stationary once you have located them where you wish for the proper gear.

At the base of the shifter, where the attachment bolt is located, you will probably find a plastic wingnut of some kind. Some have a small wire bale, some only a slotted bolt head, large enough to be turned with a dime. The purpose of these special attachment bolts is to allow the rider to tighten the shifter arm if it moves by itself (in response to cable tension), or loosen it if so tight that shifting is difficult.

b) If the shifter is not causing the chain slippage, it is possible that the derailleur is at fault. Usually, in this case, it is a problem of a changer out of alignment, and the alignment of "limiting" screws must be adjusted. (See below.)

3. Your chain falls off the smallest sprocket, or jumps over the largest sprocket into the spokes, or won't quite move up enough to engage the largest sprocket, or down the freewheel to stay on the smallest. *The solution:*

a) Remember when I was explaining the simple operation of a derailleur, and I mentioned that it was of course necessary to limit the chain's side-to-side movement to the exact extent of the freewheel, to keep the chain from falling off in either direction? Well, if one or both of your "chain-limiting adjustment screws" are misaligned, you will have problems with your chain.

b) If the chain leaps over the largest sprocket, or cannot quite seat itself on this sprocket, your low gear chain-limiting screw must be adjusted.

(Some derailleurs have a tiny "L" for low gear, and "H" for high gear stamped beneath the appropriate limiting screw.) Turning the screw clockwise with your small screwdriver will lessen the derailleur's movement, and therefore the chain's, in the direction of the largest sprocket. This will keep you from over-jumping the sprocket and hitting the spoke guard plate or spokes. Determine the degree of screw adjustment necessary by putting your bike on its back or in a stand, spinning your pedals and shifting. Turning the screw counter-clockwise will of course allow the chain greater freedom of movement toward the largest sprocket.

c) Adjustment of your derailleur for proper chain action on the smallest sprocket can be accomplished by turning the high gear limiting screw as necessary.

4. Your derailleur moves in response to you pulling back on the shifter (tightening the cable), but will not return to its original position when the shifter is moved forward again. *The solution:*

a) The problem could be, but probably isn't, a very dirty derailleur. The spring in the changer, if really loaded up with road grease, or frozen by rust, will hold the changer in one place no matter the shifter and cable movement. If this is so, clean and lubricate the entire derailleur, as described above.

b) Each time I've seen the problem of a derailleur which won't budge, the solution has been to lubricate the cable. I mentioned earlier, in the discussion of brake cables, that a broken cable housing will allow water inside. This can freeze in winter, or cause rust any time of the year. So repair or replace cracked cable housing, and lubricate the dry cable with light oil to free it from sticking.

5. Your chain slips - not to another sprocket - but while on the same cog. *The solution:*

This has happened to me only once, and was not the fault of the derailleur. (I cover the problem here, however, because most people think at first that it is the derailleur.) The reason for my slippage was worn out sprocket teeth on the smallest cog in the rear. They didn't look all that rounded to me, but the tremendous torque applied to that little sprocket when pedalling in high gear over thousands of miles had worn it just enough. If you have this problem and determine that it isn't just a loose chain (by removing one of the links - see below in chain maintenance - or by pulling your rear axle as far back in the frame drop-outs as it will go), you may have to replace the sprocket or sprockets you normally ride in. How do you do this? It really isn't difficult, but it must be done with two tools too heavy to carry with you on the road. For this reason it is a good idea to begin very long tours with a new cluster. The following steps will guide you through freewheel sprocket replacement.

a) The disassembly may be done with or without the freewheel removed from the wheel. However, I think it is easier when apart (see above). You will need one sprocket tool if you have a vise, two sprocket tools if you do not. (These tools are merely a piece of chain riveted to the end of a steel rod - $7 per pair.)

b) Assuming you are using two sprocket tools,

place the chain of one tool around the fourth sprocket down (second to largest), wrapping the chain in a clockwise direction. In the opposite direction wrap the chain of the second tool around the first (smallest) cog. I place these tools so that the handles are only a few inches apart. This allows greater control, for the handles must be pushed toward one another to unscrew the top sprocket. A strong rider's freewheel will require a great deal of strength to disassemble, for the first two sprockets are actually tightened on the freewheel body during pedalling. (When you are using two sprocket tools be careful not to apply uneven pressure against the handles - this will cause the entire freewheel to tilt and your tools will slip off. I've never damaged the tools or cogs when this happened, but I have run my knuckles into the sprocket teeth.) On most freewheels the first two sprockets screw off the freewheel body or "core" in a counter-clockwise direction, and the three remaining cogs lift off. These last three have small lugs which fit notches in the core, and usually have spacer rings between them. Don't get the sequence mixed up when you take things apart - and with a freewheel you must also replace the sprockets with the same side up as you found them.

c) If you have a vise you can take your freewheel apart in two ways. First, grip the largest sprocket in the vise jaws, wrap the sprocket tool chain around the first cog in a counter-clockwise direction, and apply force to the handle. Then proceed with the remaining sprockets as described above.

Note: The second method (the use of a vise) requires a "freewheel-axle vise tool" ($12). This tool holds the freewheel in a horizontal position for very easy disassembly.

d) To reassemble the freewheel, merely slip the first three sprockets and their spacers onto the body, and screw and tighten the top two in place. Reverse the direction of the sprocket tools to tighten the last two cogs.

Whereas some of my friends break down their freewheel bodies completely to clean and lubricate, I have never found this necessary, or worth my time to do so. The operation requires a pin spanner wrench and tweezers, and a great deal of patience to deal with the pawls and springs and tiny bearings inside. My "road lubrication method" works well for me, and after many years, if the core goes bad, I can replace it for about $6. (Entire freewheels run from about $8.50 to $25.)

I clean my freewheel core by taking it off the wheel and laying it upside down (smallest sprocket to the ground) on newspaper. Then I flush the core with Liquid Wrench (4 oz. can - 69 cents). This is done by shooting the liquid between the dust ring and main body of the core - just inside the sprocket on the back side. Give the Liquid Wrench a few minutes to work through the bearings. Pick up the freewheel and move it to a dry piece of paper, then flush it a second time. (If the ball bearings inside the core were dirty the first newspaper will be dark with grease.) A third flushing may be necessary. Then allow the bearings to dry for a few minutes, and apply a fine, light bicycle oil.

Front derailleur

At first glance you will see that your front derailleur is more simple than the rear, but it is nevertheless woefully mistreated by insensitive riders. The damage occurs when a rider fails to move the "cage" (chain guide) away from constant contact with the the passing chain. I have actually seen cages with almost all of the inside metal arm eaten through. To keep yourself from ever ruining your derailleur cage and chain, look over the following problems and their solutions *before* a problem becomes too great.

1. You hear noise while pedalling, the sound of metal upon metal. *The solution:*

a) Don't "learn to live with it." One of the beauties of a bike is its silence. Besides, you'll soon be buying a new front derailleur and chain if you don't fix it.

b) Put your bike on a stand which elevates the rear wheel from the the ground, or flip it on its back if you're on tour, or have a friend lift the back of the bike for you. Spin the pedals, and look to see when the chain hits the cage. It will probably do so at two times - when you are in your large chainring and smallest rear sprocket, and again in your small chainring and largest cog in the rear. (More often than not the most severe damage is done to the inside arm of the cage.)

c) Once you determine where your chain is rubbing, look to see if the cage is perfectly parallel with the chainring. If not, loosen the clamp bolt and turn the derailleur until it is so, being careful not to shift its position up or down on the seat tube. This could end your trouble. If it doesn't, or if the cage is parallel to the chainring to begin with, locate the high and low gear adjusting screws.

d) If the rubbing takes place while you are on your large chainring, adjust the high gear screw: only an eighth of a turn does wonders in derailleur work, so be careful not to overdo it. Turning the screw counter-clockwise will allow the cage to move out farther from the derailleur body. Adjust the screw until the chain moves freely during pedalling. However, you may have caused another common problem - the chain falling off the large front sprocket when shifting up from the smaller chainring. Test for this problem

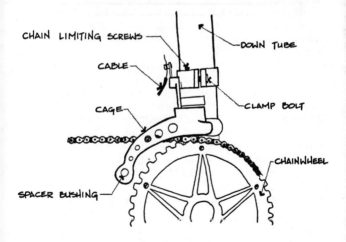

FRONT DERAILLEUR

by shifting a few times, and if the chain does fall off try the high gear adjusting screw again. If there appears no way to keep the chain from falling off and end the chain-cage contact, you will have to use your needlenose or small crescent very carefully to bend the outside arm of the cage slightly inward. But only slightly! This should be just enough to allow you once again to back out the high gear adjusting screw until the chain-cage contact while pedalling ends, and keep the chain from over-shooting the large sprocket while shifting.

e) If the chain rubs only at one spot when pedalling the problem is probably with your chainring. Just as a wheel must remain "true" to keep from rubbing against the brakes, a chainring must be true or it will slap against the sides of the cage at certain spots. Sometimes the chainring bolts - the bolts which hold the front sprockets together - come loose and must be tightened. If you have done this and the wobble is still present, check to see that your bottom bracket assembly has not worked loose. While I have never been troubled by an untrue chainring which couldn't be corrected by one of these methods. you may. If you are on tour and have no other choice I would remove the sprockets and attempt, while praying fervently, to straighten them out with light hammering. But if you are at home, or in a town with a good cycle shop, I suggest you have a good shop mechanic help you.

f) If the chain rubs against the inside arm of the cage when you are pedalling in your smaller front sprocket, work with the low gear adjusting screw in the same manner as suggested above for high gears. With this problem you may have the chain falling off on the inside of the small sprocket. If so, bend the forward tip of the inside cage away from the derailleur housing. Again, do this very tenderly.

2. Your front derailleur refuses to budge when you tug at your shifter, or fails to return to its resting position when you release the cable tension by pushing the shifter handle forward. *The solution:*

a) The answer here is the same as with your rear derailleur - a frozen cable or a very dirty changer. Lubricate the cable and changer as discussed earlier. If the derailleur must be cleaned, a more thorough job can be done if it is removed from the bike. Removal and replacement suggestions follow.

b) Critical to the proper operation of a front derailleur is its north/south position on the seat tube. Most changers work best when the outside arm of the cage is about 1/8" above the teeth of the large sprocket. However, to save myself the time and trouble of finding the proper position when I replace my front derailleur to its home on the tube, I use the metal file of my Swiss Army Knife to nick the paint on the tube just above and below the derailleur mounting clamp. This allows me to slap the changer back on the bike in no time.

I realize that my suggestion to nick your paint purposefully probably horrifies you, especially if you have a brand new bike, or one which hasn't been battered much over time. For me personally, the beauty of my bike rests in its amazing combination of form and function, not in its paint job.

c) Once you have decided whether or not to

mark your changer's location on the tube, loosen the cable anchor bolt and remove the cable.

d) Remove the bolt at the rear of the cage. Be sure to catch the small spacer brushing which rests between the cage arms, and the locknut and washer on the other side.

e) Remove the mounting clamp bolt which is furthest away from the derailleur body; loosen the other clamp bolt. Lift the derailleur from the bike.

f) Clean the changer in a pan of solvent. Brush the debris from springs and hard-to-reach areas with a toothbrush. Wipe clean and allow to dry.

g) Lubricate all springs and moving parts with oil. Remount the derailleur on the down tube; align the cage, and adjust high and low gear adjusting screws as necessary.

9.

All motorists know how much better a car seems to run when it's been washed. Well, the same goes for a bike when the chain has just been cleaned and oiled. The interminable squeaks are gone, the derailleurs move quickly up and down the sprockets, and pedalling is as smooth as silk. All this being true, why on earth don't riders clean and lubricate their chains more often? The simple answer is that most do not know how to take the chain off their bikes, and cleaning a chain in place is almost impossible.

You will need a chain removal tool (also called a "chain rivet remover") to take the chain apart. The tool costs about $3.25, and should be carried with you on tour - along with several extra links. This tool removes and replaces links, and frees "frozen" links as well.

Take a close look at your chain and you will see a series of metal side plates with rollers set between them, and held together by rivets. The plates overlap one another, and this presents us with one of the metal-upon-metal contacts in a chain which must be lubricated to prevent wear and noise. But the next point of contact is even more critical - the point where the rollers spin upon the rivets. This is where oil must be present to allow your chain its full life.

a) When a link becomes frozen, it is often as a result of dryness, and makes itself known by jumping over teeth in the sprockets, or by causing the rear derailleur to jerk forward suddenly as it passes over the tension and jockey pulleys. Elevate your rear wheel and turn the pedals to find the culprit link, and when you do, coat it with a light oil and work the link with your fingers. This may free it. If it doesn't, you'll have to use the chain tool.

b) When viewed from the side, the chain tool looks like a wide "U", with two shorter "walls" of metal between. Place the tool in front of you with the handle to the left side. Twist the handle counter-clockwise to remove the rivet "pin" from view. Now, take your chain, or preferably a few old links for practice first (many bike shops have old ones lying around which they'll give you), and place it over the first of these walls from the left. It will usually be somewhat wider than the right-hand wall. Notice, when you view your chain tool from the top, that these walls have an open space in the middle, and the chain roller rests in it, the "plates" on either side of the wall. To free a frozen link it should be placed in just this manner on the left-hand wall. Turn the tool handle clockwise until the tool rivet pin touches the chain rivet. As you turn the handle more, notice how the plates move slightly farther apart. Most often only the slightest rivet adjustment is necessary to free the link. Be sure not to push the rivet flush with the side plate, for its length is such that it should extend slightly past the plates on both sides. If it is necessary to push the rivet flush to free the link, simply turn the chain over in the tool, and apply pressure against the opposite end of the rivet.

c) To remove the chain it is necessary to drive a rivet out of one side plate, past the roller, leaving the rivet still held in place in the second side plate. This last part is the killer, and you should practice it a few times at home before having to do it on the road. (I have twice accidently driven the rivet completely free of the second plate; the first time I luckily had extra links around, the second time I did not. It took me a good half hour to wedge the free rivet back into the side plate, using the chain tool and my needlenose pliers.) Place the chain over the right-hand wall of your chain tool, and turn the handle clockwise until the tool rivet pin touches the chain rivet. Some bike shop mechanics will tell you to then turn the handle six times without fear. This is supposed to place the rivet beyond the roller, but still in the far side plate. Perhaps they suggest this so nonchalantly because bike shops use a special pliers-like tool which in one quick squeeze of the handles pushes the rivet out to the exact desired spot. For me, it's touch and go past the fifth handle turn. Beyond that point I make a quarter-turn and pull on the chain to see if it will fall free, then another quarter-turn and another tug, and so on.

d) Once my chain is free from the bike I soak it in solvent, working all links and brushing the dirtiest plates with a wire brush. Then I suspend it from a nail to dry for a half-hour, and wipe away any remaining solvent at that time. To lubricate it I place a single drop of light-weight oil on each roller, and rub the entire chain with an oiled cloth.

e) Replace the chain on the bike so that the extended rivet faces you; otherwise you'll be trying to use the chain tool backwards. When you have driven the rivet back through the roller and into the second plate you'll probably find the link to be stiff. If you do, place the link on the left-hand plate and free it, following the directions above.

Two common questions are: how do I know when I need a new chain: and, how do I know what length chain to buy? First, you need a new chain when you have an inch or more lateral play. Hold the chain in your hands, so that you are looking at the rollers, and move one hand to the right, the other to the left. An inch or more of side-play, if allowed to remain, will wear the metal teeth of the sprockets, the plastic teeth of the jockey and tension pulleys, and slap against the cage of your front derailleur.

Once you know that you do need another chain, count the number of links in your old one, and buy a new chain with exactly that number. But, should you need to fit a chain to your bike and for some reason you can't determine or trust the old length, follow this procedure. (It is not the easiest of all methods, but is in my opinion the most exact.) Put your new chain on the largest sprockets in front and rear. This should just about pull your derailleur cage until it is horizontal (your rear derailleur, that is), parallel with the chainstay. Give it some assistance by pulling the chain taut if need be, then lift the chain at the top of the chainwheel. You should have between

1/2 and 1 full link of extra chain at this point. Remove the excess links.

Finally some general observations after fifteen years of dealing with chains:

1. Chains are responsible for 90% of the dirt on a bike, due to the attraction of road grit to all the oil on the links. For this reason I keep my chain just as dry as it will permit without beginning to squeak.

2. Chains are *not* responsible for that line of grease on the inside of your right pants leg - *you* are. The chain is where it is supposed to be; learn to mount and dismount your machine properly, and use pants clips at the cuff, and you'll stay out of its way.

3. I was on a ride to Yellowstone a while back when a fellow rider told me how he didn't use oil on his chain at all. He bought blocks of paraffin instead, melted them down in a coffee can, and dipped his chain. When it dried he put it on his bike. That was such a novel idea that I had to try it, though it didn't sound all that good to me mechanically. My wife and I did try it for a while, and found it great for keeping the bike free of grease. But we finally rejected it because of the hassle melting the paraffin, the relatively short time between required dippings, and the fact that we couldn't simply add a touch of oil when developing a squeak on the road.

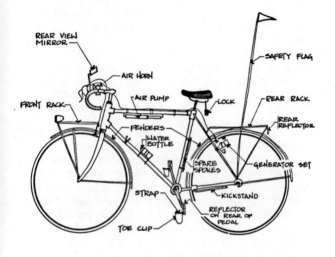

REAR VIEW MIRROR

AIR HORN

FRONT RACK

AIR PUMP

FENDERS

WATER BOTTLE

LOCK

SAFETY FLAG

REAR RACK

REAR REFLECTOR

SPARE SPOKES

GENERATOR SET

STRAP

KICKSTAND

REFLECTOR ON REAR OF PEDAL

TOE CLIP

COMMUTING BIKE

10.

In this section, I will deal with the attachment of those accessories which serious commuters will find necessary or helpful. A quick glance at a bike already set up with these items will be of great assistance when attaching your own. But in case such a bike is not nearby, and if your purchase doesn't come with directions, the following pages should be helpful.

1. Fenders:

Fenders come with four primary parts - *1)* the metal or plastic fender itself, designed to hang close to the tire and prevent the rain and road-debris from splashing up on the rider, *2)* stays - long metal arms which reach from the fenders to the front and rear wheel hubs, *3)* clamps - metal sleeves which reach around the fenders, and are attached at the other end to the brake bolts, and *4)* the nuts and bolts necessary to join the stays to the fenders and hub eyelets. Mount your fenders in the following manner:

a. Remove front and rear wheels.
b. Remove brake bolt nuts, front and rear.
c. Slide the metal clamps upon the fenders, and slip the fenders into place on the bike. Place the portion of the clamp designed to accept the brake bolt over the bolt, and tighten the brake bolt nut sufficiently to hold the fenders in place.
d. Attach the stays to the eyelets at the front fork and rear hub. Most fenders require two stays on either side, or four per wheel.
e. Position the stays so that they radiate toward the metal attaching posts on the fenders, and loosely secure these stays so that the fenders do not touch the tire. (This part of the process requires a great deal of patience, as the movement of any one stay affects all the others.)
f. Tighten brake bolt nut, both ends of stays, and replace wheels.

2. Racks:

Most front and rear racks have very simple attachment systems which require only a backing off of a brake bolt nut to hold the top rack arm, and a fastening of the two lower rack arms to the fork and rear hub eyelets. Some, however, attach at the top with the aid of two small metal bars. One bar is placed on one side of the seat stays (those thin frame tubes running from the seat post area to the rear hub), while the second bar - actually the front end of the rack itself, is positioned on the opposite side of the seat stays and bolted securely to the first bar.

The greatest difficulty with racks comes from the use of improper bolts to secure the rack arms into the eyelets. If too small a bolt is used it will

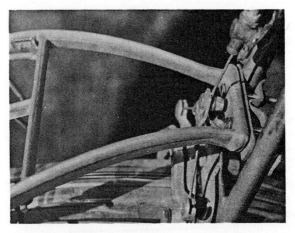

Pletscher rack mounted over center-pull brake.

Blackburn rack with brake bolt mount.

break under the strain, so mount your rack using bolts or screws which *thread* into the frame eyelets. If none are available use the largest bolt which will go through the eyelet, and secure it with a lockwasher and nut on the opposite side. (When doing this on the side closer to the freewheel you might not have enough clearance for the chain to reach the smallest cog without striking the lockwasher and nut. In this case, reverse the bolt so that the head is nearer the freewheel, and the washer and nut pointing out toward you.)

3. Flag:

The inexpensive orange safety flag is, in my opinion, the best safety feature for urban travel. Its color and movement make it highly visible even at great distances, and its height above the rider's head makes the bike's presence known even when behind an automobile.

Most flags are mounted in the rear, though I carry mine in front. But whichever location is preferred, the attachment is very simple. Merely back off the quick-release lever or wheel axle nut a couple turns, insert the metal flag mount over the axle, and re-tighten.

4. Generator Light:

All the generator systems I've seen come with directions, so I'll be brief. Basically, the support structure for the generator and taillight attach to the seat stay. The mounting location is determined by the ability of the generator wheel to rest upon the tire. This is the point where most riders foul up, and cost themselves a ruined tire. The entire face of the generator wheel must touch the tire wall: if the generator wheel strikes the tire at an angle. the metal wheel edge will eat into the tire and ruin it.

5. Toe Clips and Straps:

Toe clips attach to pedals with two small screws. These screws enter fron the front of the pedal. passing first through the toe clip. then through the front pedal housing to be held secure by a lockwasher and nut. The strap passes through the other end of the toe clip - the small hoop at the top - then down and through either side of the rear half of the pedal. Feed the strap into place so that the strap buckle meets on the outside of the pedal. otherwise the buckle will rub against the seat tube as it passes. Should the strap be a bit too long. merely twist the strap twice at the point where it is between either side of the pedal.

6. Kickstand:

Lightweight. alloy kickstands are mounted with a single bolt passing through a metal top plate positioned in the gap present behind the seat tube. and between the chainstays (thin frame tubes extending from the bottom bracket or crank hub. to the rear wheel dropout). There won't be much room present due to the fenders, so you'll have to make only quarter-turns at a time with a crescent wrench, or if you have the tools make it tight with a socket set.

7. Water Bottles:

Most water bottles are attached to the frame with two thin metal clamps, which surround both the bottle mount and frame. The ends of

Kickstand and generator light.

these clamps are connected and held in place with small screws and nuts. If the clamps are too long for your frame, wrap a couple turns of electrician's tape around the frame beneath either clamp. If the clamps are too short, you'll have to locate longer screws to reach either end, or make your own clamps with small strips of sheet metal.

Earlier I stated that I was purposefully keeping this manual short so that you can carry it with you on the road. Thus, I'll not cover air pump or mirror attachment, or run through derailleur disassembly. The first two items are self-explanatory, and the last is generally unnecessary for the commuter.

Remember that the bicycle is a relatively simple machine which can be understood and maintained even by riders with minimal mechanical aptitude. If you keep this in mind, you won't give up the first time you try to align a wheel or repack your hubs. Finally, be careful when you ride. As difficult as spokes can be, re-truing arms and legs is even trickier.

Appendix:

Bicycle

Mail Order

Catalogues

properly maintained — your bike will last you a lifetime.

Bikecology
P.O. Box 66909
Los Angeles, CA 90066

Lickton's Cycle City
31 0 Lake Ct.
Oak Park, Ill. 60302

Palo Alto Bicycles
171 University Ave.
P. O. Box 1276
Palo Alto, CA 94302

Bike/Ski Warehouse
215 Main Street
New Middleton, Ohio 44442

Sierra Specialities
1850 Bonneville Ave.
Reno, Nevada 89503

JR Touring Cycles
P.O. Box 34127
Bethesda, MD

Burley Design Cooperative
15 S. 6th Street
Cottage Grove, OR 97424

Flying Dutchman, Ltd.
Dept. "K", P.O. Box 20352
Denver, Colorado 80220

Notes

Notes

Notes

Notes

Notes

Another Book by Dennis Coello

Living on Two Wheels
The Complete Guide to Buying, Commuting and Touring

Living on Two Wheels is a detailed work designed to expose the unknown uses of the bike. Dennis Coello, who has used the bicycle as his sole means of transportation for the past 5 years, shows that the bike can be used as a replacement for the automobile in a myriad of ways. To aid the reader in his or her quest to adapt the bicycle for daily living needs, Coello provides extensive lists of all bike accessories and tools needed for a given purpose plus a comparison of the available products in today's market.

Dennis Coello writes feature articles for cycling magazines, including "Bicycling Magazine". His biking experience includes an around the world biking trip, yearly touring by bike in such places as the Rocky Mountains, and current directing of bicycle clubs and clinics.

Sixteen years ago, Dennis climbed aboard a Raleigh 3-speed and took off for Canada with no biking experience to prepare him for the trip. This is the book he wishes he had possessed then.

Size: 6"x 9"
Pages: 220
ISBN: 0-89496-034-2
Price: $5.95
Cover: Five color
Illus: Numerous detailed drawings
     and photos

Order from your local bookstore or send $6.75 (total cost including postage) to:

> Order Dept.
> Ross Books
> P.O. Box 4340
> Berkeley, Calif.
> 94704